A BABBLE OF OBJECTS

POETRY

The Kiss of Walt Whitman Still on My Lips
How to Kill Poetry
Road Work Ahead
Mute
This Way to the Acorns
St. Michael's Fall

FICTION

The Last Deaf Club in America
The Kinda Fella I Am
Men with Their Hands

NONFICTION

From Heart into Art: Interviews with
Deaf and Hard of Hearing Artists and Their Allies
Notes of a Deaf Gay Writer: 20 Years Later
Assembly Required: Notes from a Deaf Gay Life
Silence Is a Four-Letter Word: On Art & Deafness

DRAMA

Whispers of a Savage Sort and
Other Plays about the Deaf American Experience
Snooty: A Comedy

AS EDITOR

QDA: A Queer Disability Anthology
Among the Leaves: Queer Male Poets on the Midwestern Experience
Eyes of Desire 2: A Deaf GLBT Reader
When I Am Dead: The Writings of George M. Teegarden
Eyes of Desire: A Deaf Gay & Lesbian Reader

A BABBLE OF OBJECTS

POEMS

RAYMOND LUCZAK

FOMITE PRESS
Burlington, VT

IN GRATITUDE

The author is most grateful to these wonderful souls who've helped in ways large and small with this book over the last eleven years: John Lee Clark, David Cummer, and Anthony Santos. He is appreciative of Jon Marcus's verification of the T. S. Eliot quote, and of the kind words by Bryan Borland and Emily Van Kley. He is equally thankful to Marc Estrin and Donna Bister at Fomite Press for their support of this book at its finish line.

COPYRIGHT

A Babble of Objects: Poems
Copyright 2018 © Raymond Luczak

Cover Design: Mona Z. Kraculdy
Author Photo: Raymond Luczak

All rights reserved. No part of this book may be reproduced in any form or by any means without the prior written consent of the publisher, except in the case of brief quotations used in reviews and certain other noncommercial uses permitted by copyright law.

ISBN-13: 978-1-944388-59-1
Library of Congress Control Number: 2018947125

A Fomite Press First Edition

It is only in the world of objects
that we have time and space and selves.
— T. S. Eliot

for

Scott Holl

ACKNOWLEDGMENTS

These poems, many of which were visually restructured for this collection, first appeared in these periodicals and anthologies:

Assaracus: "Calendar Centerfold" and "In the Guns Section."
ByLine: "'Apostrophe'."
Chiron Review: "Doorknobs."
Clackamas Literary Review: "The Rest of Us" (originally titled "Objects").
Crab Orchard Review: "MP3."
Deaf Echo: "Keyboard" and "Measuring Tape."
FEEL Magazine: "Coils in a Mattress."
Filling the Void: A Selection of Humanist and Atheist Poetry (Jonathan MS Pearce, ed.; Onus Books): "Crucifix" and "The Other Bible."
Glitterwolf: "Scalpel in Biology" and "Tweezers."
Impossible Archetype: "Box of Tissues" and "Toothpaste Tube."
It's About Time: A Main Street Rag Anthology (Kathie Giorgio, ed.; Mint Hill Books): "Baby Shoe."
Kiss-Fist: "P.A. Parrot" and "Scanner."
Magma 69: "Bookcase," "Hearing Aide" (originally titled "What She Can't Hear"), and "Mobile."
Main Street Rag: "Atom."
The Q Review: "Cotton Sheets."
SCAB: "Mouthwash Gestapo."
Solidago Journal: "Chimney."
Sweater Weather Magazine: "Pillows."
The Tactile Mind: "Drafts."
Wordgathering: "Manuscript Tattoos."

The poem "Box of Tissues," first published in *Impossible Archetype*, was nominated for the Best of Net 2017.

This book wouldn't have been possible without the generous assistance of the John Engman Memorial Poetry Scholarship at the Loft Literary Center, enabling the author to attend Jude Nutter's class "Advanced Poetry: The Sum of Its Parts." He is most grateful to his classmates for their insightful feedback: Jevin R. Boardman, Alice Duggan, Bart Galle, Patrick Cabello Hansel, James Arch Larson, Leslie Matton-Flynn, and LeRoy Sorenson.

CONTENTS

The Other Bible 1

BATHROOM

Barbershop Quartet 5
Tweezers 6
Scale 7
Toothpaste Tube 8
Mouthwash Gestapo 9
The Grout Sisters 10
Hairbrush 11
Box of Tissues 12

SCHOOL

Calendar Centerfold 15
White Chalk 16
Bubblegum 17
Glue 18
Scalpel in Biology 19
Metaphors 20
First Dictionary 21
Similes 22
Marbles 23

BEDROOM

Mobile 27
Watch Bands in a Box 28
'Apostrophe' 29
Cotton Sheets 30
Retouching Yourself 31
Pillows 32
Manuscript Tattoos 33
V i b r a t o r 34
Bobby Pin 35
Coils in a Mattress 36

BUILDING

Measuring Tape 39
Chimney 40
Brick Wall 42
Doorknobs 43
Scanner 44
Bookcase 45
The Architect's Lamp 46
Photograph Taken Off a Wall 47

HOME

MP3 51
Mirrorball 52
Iron 53
Aspirin 54
Stock Pot 55
Collar 56
Universal Remote Control 57
Drafts 58
Baby Shoe 59

OFFICE

Harem of Keys 63
Keyboard 64
Disinfectant 65
Hearing Aide 66
Batfan 67
Stapler Dog 68
Magazine in a Dentist's Waiting Room 69
Credit Card Girls 70
Solar-Powered Calculator 71

SHOPS

P.A. Parrot 75
Thumbtacks 76
Books of Verse 77

Dressing Room Mirror 78
In the Guns Section 79
Mercenary Heels 80
Cane-Cane 81
Threads 82
Gloves 83
Old Man Concrete 84
Junk Mail 85

LANDFILL

Noise 89
Fertilizer 90
Crucifix 91
Garbage Bag 92
Washing Machine 93
Cathode Ray Tube 94
Atom 95
The Rest of Us 96

THE OTHER BIBLE

Us objects didn't have to believe in anything.
We had no need for passing stories late at night
from one generation to the next.
That's how long we'd lived.

Artifacts excavated in archeological digs
were our ancestors, broken
and catalogued into tiny white boxes.
Our lives used to be so simple.

Now created in seconds on assembly lines,
we've been made to feel like heathen.
We are savages in need of enlightenment.
Factory workers repeat stories that confuse us:

one day their Savior will return,
restoring peace among His Chosen People.
But their true Messiah's already arrived.
His name is Money, and he brings war.

BATHROOM

BARBERSHOP QUARTET

Onstage underneath the bathroom sink,
we cleaners hold forth with our white suits
and bright vests labeled with stripes
spelled out in English and *Español*.

Our voices swirl melodies so brisk
they could scour a toilet bowl clean.
Our moustaches are waxed with dribbles
of chemicals no one can pronounce.
Our rosy cheeks are powdery with bluster.
Having no phosphates in our trills sucks.

Our songs no longer carry in the sewage
biling out into the rivers. No matter
how people try to make us safer, we'll hum
all night long until our throats burn.

TWEEZERS

I spend too much time behind the mirror.
There's never enough sun among band-aids,
hydrogen peroxide, and cotton balls—
such lugubrious nincompoops,
showing off their fatness for all to see.
My moisturized skin shines as if tanned in chrome.
It's a good distraction from all my flaws.
My inner thighs are getting rusty,
and I used to be so damn proud of my skin!
Sometimes it hurts to squeeze my scummy legs,
the inner soles of my feet sanded raw,
a grip to pull embedded hangnails out
or grasp around an errant nostril hair.
Oh, please. This is not what I've signed up for.

SCALE

I love fat people the way they love cake,
guzzle diet sodas loaded with artificial sweeteners
that deposit so neatly in cellulite folds,

    and stuff their mouths with burgers and fries
    from the nearest fast food joint while
    they watch TV shows filled with people

too beautiful to ignore and hate.
I sit next to the toilet where I hear
the grunts and groans of their weight.

    I love it when I feel their beads of sweat
    hit my forehead as they balance themselves
    on my shoulders. I go cross-eyed with numbers.

Sometimes their tears rain all over my face.
I want to tell them over and over again
how beautiful they are just as they are.

    Without them I would've been a nobody,
    a worthless piece of junk made in China,
    an impulse cheapie in a no-name store.

I'm a gawk-eyed teenage girl hiding her flat boobs
behind books, or a pimply-faced boy too skinny
to get picked for any sports. No,

    I don't deserve to be a nobody.
    Fat people may hate me, but I'm so full
    of love for them I might just collapse.

TOOTHPASTE TUBE

I'm a mermaid, shimmering scales
                every morning for your bad breath.
I like it when you pinch my tail
                and roll my fin even tighter.

                              I love how my hips flesh out.

If I were human, you wouldn't look at me twice.
        I'd be a lumpy secretary with a bad perm
spending evenings alone with the TV.
        But dressed like this, I'm of the sea.

                Who cares if I won't live long? I've got you.

As long as I fill your mouth with my breath,
        your wife will remain lusty for my kisses
you spread out atop your toothbrush.
        She'll never know my name, but she loves me.

                    Polygamy couldn't be any cleaner.

MOUTHWASH GESTAPO

We're clinically proven to have no feelings.
    Our blue-green bodies clack awake
the second you slide open the mirror door.
    We've been trained to rustle up
the germs hiding in the caves of your teeth,
    but they won't come out. They've heard
stories of their relatives rinsed out
    without warning. We break forth in song:
heartrending anthems of our fatherland
    and the virtues of hygienic purity.
As one by one succumbs to our patriotism,
    we round them up for the sink's drain and push
out in a big fall. You'll spit out the last of us,
    and smile. Today will be a good one for America.

THE GROUT SISTERS

It didn't take the guy   with a cigarette hanging
from his mouth long to squeeze us
between white tiles.   We wove our fingers
tight as we could. We were now sisters.
Then came our first hailstorm   from the showerhead.
We thought we were going to die.
Then another man came in   and soaped naked!
Sometimes we forgot to zip up our lips,
and the brown grime   covered us.
We were the color of embarrassment.
But we couldn't wait for   his wife's toothbrush
scratching cruddy mildew across our faces.
Then we'd dry, dreaming   of her perfect husband
washing all over and whistling just for us.

HAIRBRUSH

Each time she pushes me through her hair, I moan.
I may have only one hand, but oh many fingers!
My plastic nails have been clawed to their roots.
It is always a thrill to scratch her scalp.
The heat from her head is like the sun.
I excavate dandruff like an archaeologist.
My palm is a temporary burial ground.
It looks like the sprawling head of Medusa.
Sometimes she plucks at me above the toilet.
She leaves me, covered with trapped hairs, in a drawer.
I've perfected the art of dreaming day-long silences.
When she opens my drawer, I awaken with hope.
Will she disentangle my heart-strands today?
No matter: she's forever my queen of hair.

BOX OF TISSUES

I'm a dreamer with a laundry list of things
I hate. Snot is one of them.
I wish I could hide myself from their hands

but they know how to dig into me,
ripping out a tiny sheet of puffy dream
just to wipe their dribbling noses.

When they don't need me, it's beautiful
when dust settles on my shoulders.
I feel like an angel blessed with wings.

Among clouds I float all day long,
warmed by dreams of their perfect health,
where their rooms fill with contented silences.

Dreaming and waking
is a constant war of letting go.
I long for a time when no one needs

me.

SCHOOL

CALENDAR CENTERFOLD

The teacher hates me, but boys and girls love the checkerboard style of my numbered skirts. No one cares what top I'm wearing that month. They check my grid when they come in the room, and stare at me when the teacher looks down. I am their first schoolyard crush. I promise gift-filled Christmas breaks, Easterly respites, languorously hot summer vacations, and rapid-fire weekends free of homework. I dare blush, the lucky recipient of their stolen glances. I count their dreams. I am their first kiss of mortality. One day they will grow up and find me gone. The schoolyard's no longer the world it was.

WHITE CHALK

    .... The blackboard was our favorite ice pond
    .... where we shrieked as we skated trails of words,
    ..... equations, and numbers, all meaningless.
    .... We were all pulled along for the ride.
    .... Kids covered their ears in pain.
    .... We giggled at their wincing expressions.
    .... Their teacher didn't seem to mind so much.
When she was done, we hung on for our lives,
    ..... fearing the eraser's power to wipe.
    .... These days we see the computer's smug glare
    .... projected onto a whiter pond that hangs
    .... immaculately, a speck-free masterpiece.
    ..... No one warned us about the true winter
    .... of our lives, the powder of our tears.

BUBBLEGUM

The first part of my life was just AWESOME.
I lived SEVENTEEN days in saliva
before the girl POPPED me out of her mouth
and stuck me RIGHT HERE under her desk chair.
Dust soon covered my face. I couldn't sneeze.
I kept WAITING for her to remember.
Didn't SEVENTEEN days count for something?
But *NOOO*, her legs went TRA-LA-*LA* in class.
Sometimes she dropped her pen and picked it up.
But she NEVER looked me right in the eye.
What kind of a friend was she anyways?
But then I started HEARING other gums
sniffling about in the neighborhood. WEIRD.
At last alone in dust, we all achooed.

GLUE

my lungs are coated with a gooey white__it's sometimes hard to breathe naturally__with that stupid hospital orange cap__ over my one nostril that dries mucus__my plastic skin is a hospital gown__my butt's got dumb UPC tattoo stripes__I've never understood why I was made this way__these people try to doctor me__by stabbing needles into my nostril__they puncture open to allow in air__all without anesthesia or warning__surgery needn't be this barbaric__they're already squeezing me upside down__trying to breathe is a brutal science

SCALPEL IN BIOLOGY

Every year I hear them go through their *eeeuw*s
when these dead frogs lie, slightly frozen.
　　I'm good for only one thing, so I glint
　　under the fluorescent lights.
　I have to hide chuckles at how I'm held.
　Adolescence never had this much fear
　　or trepidation. My tip pokes deeper,
　　a hesitation into the unknown
lining, the unseparated organs
　soon to be carved out and pinned to a slab.
　　My handler is less afraid with his moves.
It's a joy that scalpels sliver off.
　　　We're no longer student and scalpel.
　　　Deep inside the body's chaos do we sing clarity.

METAPHORS

We cannot tell you the truth straight ahead.
We have no clue what cold hard facts should mean.
We are too flighty and too artistic.
We are unreliable weather vanes.
No wind can tell us which way to forecast.
Roads and rivers earn our lifelong disdain.
We buff our nails until they mirror us,
ignoring those world's-end-is-near phone calls.
Fort Knox can't breach our imaginations.
We'd post their security codes online.
We spend our days avoiding our cousins,
those similes too proud of their breeding.
We've indulged in clever chatter too long
to stop. We are children who won't grow up.

FIRST DICTIONARY
The American Heritage Dictionary, Second College Edition

     You've lived with me for three decades,
but I must give you away to sleep.
     I haven't stroked your dog-eared pages in years.

     You've sat in the crate of my bookshelves,
watching me and hoping
I'd call you up one more time onto my lap
and rub your belly while searching
for that perfect word.

     You've never left my side through eight moves
in three cities. You helped me
define the loss of friendship and
the many permutations of love.
     Those assholes made me cry. You made me a poet.

     Heaven will be filled with dogs I've loved,
and you've lived the longest.
     May your hard back turn into wings.
     My heart's a tail that never stops.

SIMILES

We're like nobody you know,
and if you did know us well,
you'd find us boring.

We keep our houses clean.
We are strict nine-to-fivers.
We crave paperwork.

We don't even gossip.
We go to the water cooler
and come right back to our desks.

We keep our inboxes empty.
We may be busy, but please,
dear writers, stop by and say hello.

Please lie about us with something
more exciting than our blank lives.
That would be our biggest thrill.

"Like a lion"? Why, that would fill us
with dreams of Africa far beyond
our paltry computer screens.

Otherwise we're nobodies on the train.

MARBLES

We knew how to multiply in their hands.
We were once treasured and bartered like coins
in their stock exchange out on the playground.
These boys, boasting already of manhood,
across the dirt and flicked their thumbs up
to toss us far into their kick-dug hole.
Sometimes we landed perfectly. Or not.
We never cared. We were happy to be
cradled and rolled across their sweat-moist palms.
The more beautiful and exotic ones
among us were like rubies and sapphires,
always fingered in pockets while in class.
Left in jars and boxes to be sorted,
we miss these boys, now outgrown in the world.

BEDROOM

MOBILE

I am a ballet dancer on a diet

    of wind that tumbleweeds from the window.

        The ceiling is my stage.

    Each spin of shape is a lover's sweet sigh,

impossible to grab, like fireflies,

    a dusk of summers to ache for when old.

        Let my rustles startle you from nightmares

    of horses thundering through your bedroom.

Question me as to whether I did hear their hooves.

    I guide you back to the right path

        laced with undulating bright-red poppies.

    Child, you were always my best audience.

Sleep, for you can never have enough dreams.

    One day you'll forget the suitcase of me.

WATCH BANDS IN A BOX

Every morning we awaken with our colors awash with a sweet residue of your sweat underside. We are of many races: fluoroelastomer, nylon, leather, Milanese loop, and stainless steel links. The wedges of our souls have been engineered to slip in and lock into your smartwatch, already laser-blinking each pump of vein.

Each of us have experienced a full day of you: tense phone calls, lunchtime banter, grunt-filled half-hour on the sofa while you watch TV, lazy chuckles to be your nameless best friend. We are happy to be your nameless best friend. Our souls deliriously clammy from cradling your wrist if only for one day to cherish.

'APOSTROPHE'

It hangs sweetly in the air, its tail poised for action.

Something must be said for contraction:
"can not" becomes *can't*, "do not" becomes *don't*.

The hangnail is cushioned, sheathed. Its dagger is firmly in place.
In the little wars between lovers,
the tail divides, maps out territories:

this is Adrienne's,   that's Jack's.

No, the tail is an index finger

admonishing our desires to possess,
to claim as our own.

Alone, it is innocuous. Paired, we feel the power of waiting.

COTTON SHEETS

Every night is the same. These two strip and slip into embrace

as we rise, slither across their tangled bodies, collecting each

precious bead of tenderness and lust, moistening our parched

tightly-woven skins. When we plants were young, we grew in the

sun, scorching our whiteness and sucking water with our roots.

We could never drink enough. Our plucking was a thirst turned

inside out. Our veins were twisted into skin not ours. Their

skins against ours are sweet coupling. When they both grunt and

groan, we sigh and moan as sweat sprinkles down from their

brows to ours. They'll never know what a rain dance love is.

RETOUCHING YOURSELF

When choosing a [picture] for hookup apps,
your ugliness is a <3breaking problem.
Allow me to [delete-key] the unsightly sags
under your [red] eyes, and your double chin too.
I like to prance my magic [finger-wand] around,
crop hips too wide [pinch-in] for a grid of thumbnails,
apply band-aids [airbrush] to deep forehead creases,
lighten moles, and accentuate [shadow] breasts.
I am an app [icon]: pure algorithm, the golem,
the Dorian Gray, the Fountain of Youth
written to disguise your flaws. Break my code,
and you run the risk of learning what
I've long known: your defects are perfect.
Your fear of beauty [<3<3<3] is the reason why I exist.

PILLOWS

((You two are my plump Atlases,
holding up the weight of my head.)
(Ache outweighs osmium every time.)

(You two are full of whispers I imagine
coming from him on the nights he'd stayed
long enough to kiss me good-bye.)

(You two are made of polyester muscle,
tagged with faded product warnings.)
(I didn't know that love could be toxic.))

((Your twin shoulders are strong,
cradling my chin as I wrap around you two
and squeeze hard the ghost of him

out into the night air where he floats
like a goose down feather oceans away.)

(((Carry me home, for I've lost my way.))))

MANUSCRIPT TATTOOS

Each story is a tattoo that I show and tell
    in a bar on Saturday nights. My body
will accumulate stories deeper than ink.

I inject the million-plus colors of memory
    into the black limbs of letters and pray
that others will dream the same way.

I try to be precise when I puncture the onionskin
    paper. Their blank stares do not shed a tear.
Like mine, their hearts are under anesthesia.

I have only scars. The ink of me has dried out.

VIBRATOR

I don't mind being her secret friend. }{ I'm perfectly fine left alone, snuggled }{ among her panties and bras. }{ I suppose I'm every man's fantasy, going deeper }{ where he's never gone. I feel so full }{ with the AA batteries inside me. She presses }{ my joy button: I quiver off buzzes. }{ It's very loud and worse than white noise. }{ My silicone skin throbs. Faking orgasms }{ gives me headaches, I wish she would just stop }{ moaning out his name, stop weeping for him, }{ he was the type to drink and get high anyway, }{ oh turn me off, and find someone else better, }{ someone kinder with a tender buzz.

BOBBY PIN

When Louise Brooks pranced in the film *Pandora's Box*,
showing off her helmet hair, its curls sharp
and defiant, as she broke one heart after another,
not quite comprehending the power of her sex,
I thought my future was made. I held the wavy spear
of immorality by keeping my woman's bobbed hair
in place. She drank bad whiskey and laughed
as jazz smoked and snaked through speakeasies.
Then she dared to lift her skirt for a Yale fella
who brushed me off. She forgot to look for me
when I fell into a crack of hardwood floor.

                I still call out her name.

COILS IN A MATTRESS

We are ^reshaped^ under ^factory\ lights^
and spend the ^rest\ of\ our\ lives^ ~in\ the\ dark~.
Our ^padded^ voices are muffled along.
The first time a person ~plops~ on our heads
without a ^warning^ in a mattress store
is a shock we ^never^ recover from.
We are ~never~ young and carefree again.
With each ^groan^ of weight we overhear grunts
of ~fuck~ and ^sighs\ of\ dream^. The routine grows
tiresome as we realize there's nothing new.
Our minds numb ~the\ sensations~ of forced hurt
when owners ^toss\ us\ out^ for a new bed.
We long for the day when our padding tears,
^exploding^ sunlight's ~dust~ and our first ^rust^.

BUILDING

MEASURING TAPE

1. All my numbers lie. It doesn't matter
2. how long I stretch from here to the couch
3. or how far I reach from floor to ceiling.
4. I hide secrets of irregular walls,
5. the patchy crookedness of hardwood floors,
6. and the lopsidedness of my body.
7. A few millimeters off on one end
8. can multiply into two-by-fours
9. that are readjusted and sawn
10. too short until the damned revelation
11. arrives at the very last possible minute.
12. The joke is that no one blames me. Ever.
13. That they still try building houses is sad.
14. It's far better and simpler to make do.

CHIMNEY

This chimney's rickety, old,
   and cranky as hell.
      It leaks out heat now and then
              before it drifts
    off into the arms of ice
   waiting to embrace the ghost of my wife
    trapped in the attic
      when the roof caught fire.
  Yeah. This house is falling apart,
        no longer up to code but left
  for dead like all else
around here. So far no one's
   come knockin' for me right outta here.
    Not even my kids.
  Not a bad deal if you ask me.
      They don't know where I am.
     Besides, in those shelters
thieves flock worse than cockroaches.
Each night I collect thick phone books
    and watch numbers burn.
   Who knew perfect lives could crumble
         so easily?
Ashes nudge me awake at dawn.
    Just me and this chimney crackling,
  whispering how

    one day its soot will become wind,
   how I'll be left standing, skeleton-like,
  when its last brick falls
    to the sound of my kids
   acting shocked
that my will has turned to dust.

BRICK WALL

When bricklayers wiped away our mortar tears, it was the last time we'd felt pain. Then we got sheeted in plaster and drywall.

We spent decades eavesdropping, marveling at the cruel things you said to your kids.

One day your realtor decided you'd sell better if they scrubbed off the pimples of mold and pancaked paint from our faces.

Powdery with the color of autumn leaves, we remember the endless gray winters, shivering and aching for a little warmth, just like you now with your kids grown up and gone.

Kids will knock you down first. They always do. Our amber-lined veins are tears in fossil.

DOORKNOBS

As fingers twist our stiff heads and necks,
we are worn smooth by implosions of rage.
We are the worse for wear from verbal abuse.
We interpret the languages of touch
in dialects too complex for linguists.
No one appreciates our finesses
or our explanations of how hinges,
white-knuckled, hang-glide in rust and stilled air.
It's no wonder that their wives feel so screwed
with each slam housequaking the stodgy frame.
Even the door blames us enough to spread
big lies to neighbors whose eyes pry and sigh.
We will surely die stuck and discarded
at weddings no one remembers to attend.

SCANNER

I don't do well with smudgy fingerprints.
Everything you give me is a matter
of life or pixels: how cheap should I be
when I look up-down with my Day-Glo eye
each photograph and magazine picture?

How much fidelity can you endure
when I blink my eye slowly to reveal
my view of what you've always remembered
there on your screen. I am a sheet of glass,
peeling away your perceptions for mine.
I rage against DPI in color.
You deserve more precision than I can give.

One day your memory will fail. So will mine.
How strange you'd still entrust me with so much.

BOOKCASE

                      In a former life I was
                      a thousand-year redwood.
     Before I was trimmed
       and planed to spec,
                 I was a glimmer
                 in the mind's eye
      of my creator blessed
    with ruler and hammer.
                 He's gone now.
                 Others have painted over
     my true self with color.
      No one will ever see
                the likes of me,
                tall and wide,
       arms deep enough
for dreams made of hands.

THE ARCHITECT'S LAMP

Turning on my light drops
        a heavy stone
into water stilled after a long frost.

    My glow radiates waves and
           throbs upward
    to the ceilinged white sky.

        The land below pulses
           a steady glow
    as sharpened pencils glide
        across the water
marked with T-squares and printed out
                again.

      The architect papers his angular
inshore lines with precise millimeters.

      I shimmer lilies around
          his halo.

    This is where he will build
     the cabin's foundation
    entrenched into the deep
      guts of the earth.

It's still theory as he turns off my light
     and leaves the light on
       in his dreams.

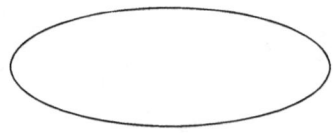

PHOTOGRAPH TAKEN OFF A WALL

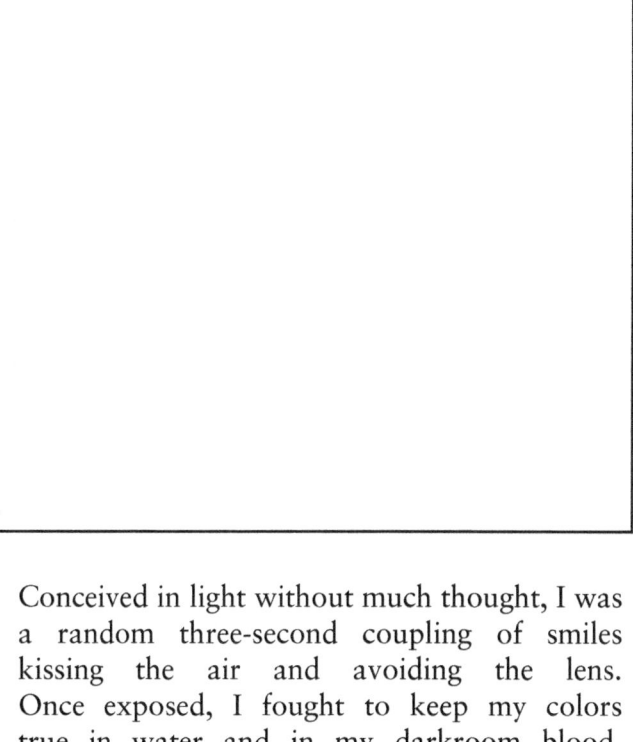

Conceived in light without much thought, I was a random three-second coupling of smiles kissing the air and avoiding the lens. Once exposed, I fought to keep my colors true in water and in my darkroom blood. My movements hobbled inside frame and glass. Sunlight archived my permanent blindness. I sensed furtive glances and listened for their stories of the day I was snapshot. Nothing they said jibed with what I recall. Sometimes I wondered if they were senile. I breathed very slowly so not to fog the mirror crystal-eyed to all but me. I shall remember the exactitude of them.

HOME

MP3

On 23 October 2001, the day when the iPod was announced

Stoke the fire of my words into a puff ... of smoke slithering into the dark unknowns ... beyond the cochleas into the polished canals ... deep into the halves of gray matter ... where spongy earbuds clap together ... like fingers snapping on automatic pilot ... to reverb a few decibels louder than bombs ... DJ'ing from one twitchy turntable of doubt ... to the next kiss until the morning after ... filled with at least 5,000 choices of how ... to play awkwardness with a hapless smile ... Clichés become another menu option ... Who knew there could be so many? ... My soul is compressed but I listen pure ... with my heart a quick scroll wheel ... away from skipping the song we never sang ... Nothing but sad love songs coos into ... the whiteness bleeding out of my ears.

MIRRORBALL

Spinning every night has gotten tiresome.
It's a damn miracle that I don't have vertigo.
I've got infrared vision and bionic ears.
I can see and hear all that goes on
in the shadows and black lights.
I cast glittery hopes everywhere.
Everyone watches me when they're not busy
texting just to look important.
It's the same old story: girl wants guy,
guy wants someone else, girl's still alone.
Hey, girl, come dance under me anyway.
You'll remember this song
one day when you're in the car,
    feeling old and fat
        with a squalling baby and wondering
           what the hell happened tonight.

IRON

Fill ○ your ○ slick ○ esophagus ○ with ○ water
and ○ let ○ your ○ electrical ○ chest ○ expand ○ with ○ heat.
You ○ know ○ how ○ to ○ control ○ your ○ rage,
grilling ○ steam ○ holes ○ in ○ once-perfumed ○ collars.
Each ○ breath ○ of ○ yours ○ is ○ a ○ scald ○ of ○ cotton
that ○ hisses ○ wrongdoings ○ and ○ fitful ○ dreams
like ○ a ○ feral ○ cat ○ squirreled ○ away ○ in ○ the ○ closet.
Betrayals ○ shouldn't ○ come ○ so ○ easily.
Feel ○ her ○ invisible ○ cigarette ○ smoke
arise ○ in ○ his ○ arid ○ exhalations,
all ○ helium ○ leaden ○ with ○ lies.
See ○ how ○ quickly ○ his ○ tears ○ evaporate
when ○ he ○ promises ○ not ○ to ○ see ○ her ○ again.
Each ○ wrinkle ○ of ○ his ○ begs ○ forgiveness.
He • will • steam • to • hell • inside • his • collar.

ASPIRIN

Under the unbroken seal
of our childproofed caps,
we await the uncorking.

We were born to speed up
enzymes, color blood cells,
and leap across synapses.

O so many of us would love
to race against each other
down the squirmy waterfall,

down to the stomach's cesspool.
Our oxygen adds acid bubbles
and we giggle when it tenses

into swallowing stabs of pain.
We white crumbs mesh against
each other in spasms.

We win the emergency room's
grim respect as they pump
out the bog of helplessness.

We do not have a conscience.
We were measured to run against
time, the power of the stomach.

STOCK POT

I'm a beer-bellied biker tattooed with burnt stains.
                I plop my plumber's ass on the stove
after she's tanked me with water.
                Then that smokin' blue throttle of propane!
I'm always happy when she expects me
           to fart bubbles while I wear my lid-cap.
She works so damn hard to feed her kids.

I'm a long-haired mutt best crated away.
             The only time I don't mind the way I look
is when she holds her palms against my love handles
             and waits for my heat to evaporate,
sighs from her body trembling against me,
            just like how I'd ride my Harley-Davidson.
If only I could be retooled as flesh and bone.

COLLAR

I am every dog's curse. I am teeth to his leash of nylon. I breathe in everything he does and rein in his nose on walks. His license tags jaggle like earrings. I choke him when he darts off too quickly. I feel toothless every time I'm taken off and left on the counter when he is taken in for a bath. In that split second between floor and tub, I catch sight of my dog shaking free of my shadow on his neck.

UNIVERSAL REMOTE CONTROL

Until I am pressed, my life is useless.

My electronic boys by the TV are too busy grooming their silver sheen and showing off their LCD blink-bling.

When my beeps turn angry, a shrill fire drill, I am their mother, and they hate it.

They respond slowly as if they're too cool to admit that yeah, they have a mother.

They drop their shoulders and move, fast-forward, to selections on the Blu-Ray disc's menu as if touching a Lamborghini.

They swagger with grins of insolence.

What they don't know is that they'll die young.

All last-year models do. I soldier on.

DRAFTS

The bad ones had ~~health~~ problems.
They were doomed ~~to die together.~~
~~They were~~ [There have been] ~~so~~ many. It hurts
to remember the hopes I had for them.
I train myself not to dwell on ~~the~~ [my] dreams [.]
~~I had for each baby. So much time gone.~~
I've become a ~~cold-blooded~~ funeral director,
deciding whom to discard, whom to embalm.
I cram the ~~cheap~~ boxes with their bodies~~,~~ [.]
~~ashy orphans of my former ambition.~~
I lug their coffins over the counter.
I do not pay shipping insurance.
Workers will not give those coffins respect.
~~The cargo is just part of their dirty job.~~
In a ~~temperature-controlled~~ mausoleum,
they will each lay a stillborn corpse.
~~Preserved,~~ [T]these dead babies will haunt
the memory of the ~~awful~~ daddy I was.

BABY SHOE

Lord, I used to be thrilled like his mother
when I felt his tiny-pea toes wriggle
and then press down as he took his first steps.
I understood why people had to love
even if arguments made them forget.
I overheard talk of how I should be bronzed
so that the baby, now much older, could gauge
how far he's gone.

Please don't dip me into bronze for posterity.
My big flat ass is solid as a hoof.
My stiff skin has nicks of gray against white.
My only necklace is a striped shoelace.
Please let me watch him grow old as a century.
I haven't anything else to do.

OFFICE

HAREM OF KEYS

When wives see us jiggle, they hone their glares.
  We giggle with promises to a world
that sings of curve-hugging speeds, business trips,
  a corner office with manicured trees.
Everything far from home is vacation
  as our men stiff-lip negotiations,
number-crunch their battle plans in Excel,
  and feel their groins ache for all that's been lost.
From deep in their pockets we watch our men
  age from honeymoon exhilaration
to growing bills and family frustrations.
  We're all there to cheer them up, wives be damned.
While we may get scratched and nicked over time,
  we will never die as long as men lie.

KEYBOARD

I long to impart words all my own, but his stubby fingers do the talking. He's way too dull. I'm kaput from input. I'm a punctual email, a simple "thanks," a click on "send." Or I'm saved for later. I'm lucky if he fires an angry note to his boss. The sharp jolt of his soft taps is sometimes worth the tedium of wait. But I can't bear witness to my own life, mere words testifying that I did type. I'm not a dot-com machine. My soul's still trapped in the casket of black plastic nubs. No one knows my real name. I'm not allowed tospellitupthereonthescreen.

DISINFECTANT

I have perfected the art of   spitting.
My spittle sprays on the backs of microbes
who always giggle at my half-assed attempts.
It's an enjoyable cat-and-mouse game.
I'm a lazy feline; they scuttle for fun.
We both know that the game will resume.
It takes a human to squeeze my stiff throat,
a turkey's wattle for my battle   cry.
The sting of alcohol clears my senses
as I watch the human swipe with paper
towels that seem sterile but not quite so.
It's all good. These microbes will forgive me.
One day my sharp spit weakens and   e x p i r e s.
I'm quickly replaced. I'm only a temp.

HEARING AIDE

Hooked on the sweet flesh of her ear,
I fish in sounds that she'll be able to recognize:
the door opening, the oven timer dinging,
the ambulance about to whiz by, a dog barking.

Yet so many more things she won't be able to hear:
"Sorry, I didn't realize she was deaf and dumb."
"Hey! Can you read my lips? Like this?
Oh, wait! How about it if I turn my head like this?"
"CAN. YOU. UNDERSTAND. ME. YES?"
"Gosh. Why can't she speak if she's got hearing aids?"

No matter what sounds tumble against her eardrums,
she doesn't need me to amplify the language
of ignorance. She understands it perfectly.
Those are the times when I wish I didn't have to hear.

BATFAN

I'm perched on the veneer-backed ledge

of a short bookcase. I pretend I'm Batman,

but my four wings are laced with dust.

My mask grille is choked with a film of

grease gloved between each finger

of black metal. I constantly dream

of having the cool technology to swing

from one end to the other of

this looming cubicle metropolis,

gray, beige, and interminably dull,

an unbreakable thread that doesn't stop

as I spin through the big conference room,

shattering its window for the world

below where my biggest foes await.

STAPLER DOG

No one cares   until I show my steel fangs
snapping and   locking down hard on the bone
of white-   layered cakes that have no marrow.
Stapling   photocopies are for sissies.
I crave   the stiff meatiness of card stock
where my   gums would hurt from puncturing it.
Everything's   been recycled to death.
I want   something fresh. I want growth hormones.
I want   two-inch-thick slabs of fatty pulp.
I've never   had juices drip off my chin.
Oh, just   send me off to the slaughterhouse
before   people stop printing magazines
thinning   each month. My days are numbered.

MAGAZINE IN A DENTIST'S WAITING ROOM

My face's been acne'd from too many thumbs,

lightly licked to bend and lift the next page

full of sly advertisements and come-ons

about how to seduce your bored husband.

I swear my body will run a full-color bleed,

much darker than rivers of mascara

across the industrial-strength carpet.

I know all about these restless women

from the way they glance mindlessly straight through.

Their furtive eyes are go-to-page-numbers

as they glance at their kids and use their phones.

When their names are called, I'm quickly dumped

the same way husbands drop their mistresses.

They can't wait to see their sharpened bites gleam.

CREDIT CARD GIRLS

We've got the cushiest job in the world.
We don't have to put on lipstick or rouge.
We just lie there in the folds of purses
and wallets on a bed of throaty trills.
What you all want is our magnetic stripes.
We fake your discretionary incomes
for the thrill of getting swiped in public.
That we make love anywhere is obscene.
The most intimate details of your life
sponsor the lives of our corporate pimps.
We bankrupt your secrets to marketers.
What you make are just pitiful pennies!
We just have to remember not to laugh
the next time you escort us to the bar.

SOLAR-POWERED CALCULATOR

Every time I blink, it's money.
I feel their fingertips jabbing on my body,
and I see in their eyes a deadening
of pulse as my numbers
flash a marquee of debts.

They try again with different numbers.
I am pummeled with curse words.
Sometimes I overhear them guillotining
credit cards with brute scissors
until shards turn into dull diamonds.

The bills on the table are spread out
like beach towels on the sand. I'm topless
again in Club Med where the sun will
rejuvenate me with resolve to withstand
their glares. Dreaming is free.

SHOPS

P.A. PARROT

I've turned blind from *staring* at cars parking.
It's no accident that I am a *twit*,
an electronic bird *trapped* in its cage.
Squabbles and *silences* of families
walking beneath drift through my *cloistered* veil,
where I *ache* to shift the weight of my voice.
I *chirp*, monitored for modulation,
extorting shoppers to *listen* again
to what I've *tired* of repeating: "New sale!"
Everything's on *sale*. "Forty percent off!"
My talons are covered with *cheap* gold paint.
When the last store closes, I flex my *wings*.
Nights I practice my *sing-song* mating call
and dream of *her* returning with a song.

THUMBTACKS

We Are The Orphans No One Wants On Board
Until We're Convenient To Tack On
Photocopied Fliers Of Garage Sales,
Lost Puppies, Artist/Business Cards, And Bikes.
We've Seen How These Foster Parents Behave
When They Think No One Else Is Watching Them.
They Pick Each One Of Us Out From The Mob,
Collect Our Sad Merchandise Off The Cork,
And Force Our Happy Smiles On Their Fliers
So They Are Front And Center. They Look Good.
Yes, We're Now A Big Happy Family!!!
That Never Lasts Long. Someone Else Appears
With Sheaves Seeking Another Guitarist.
We Are All Broken Homes Pretending Whole.

BOOKS OF VERSE

Once upon a time we were nondescript.
Just the title and the author's name engraved.
Tiny expensive things.
Then untalented poets decided to hold forth.
We had to change our clothes to sell.

Now harlots gussied up
from four-color printing presses,
we're ordered to stand and pose with promises
like those hookers waiting behind big windows
in Amsterdam's De Wallen.

Our come-on hithers echo neon
when you pick us up in a bookstore.
No matter how standoffish we may appear outside,
it's the black lingerie of our text that you want.
Please disrobe our loneliness.

DRESSING ROOM MIRROR

My first year wasn't too bad. Young women
preened their bodies with fuchsia Spandex tops
in front of me, never hearing my *tsk*s
as I saw in their eyes their lost beauty
in need of reattainment at a price.

Then my store went bankrupt and I was sold
to a maternity shop. The moon glow
rising up from their wombs to their faces
quickly lost its novelty. Motherhood
was clearly not cut out for some of them.

Then I moved uptown to a place filled with
starchy pantyhose and beige walking shoes.
I've seen way too many varicose veins.
I'm forever young. You can kiss my glass.

IN THE GUNS SECTION

Hanging us upside down under bad lights, the store must think we women guns are weak. We're too petite for quarterly quotas. The blood settles in the top of our heads, squishing down on the bottoms of our eyeballs. We watch the pot-bellied humans strut up, show their IDs, and fondle the men guns posed sideways like centerfolds below us. They sprout faggot-bashing like poetry. We radar for their bedraggled housewives, their shopping carts full of squalling babies. Our keg-powdered faces aren't loud enough. Somebody, please pull our triggers and shoot those fat assholes. We've got splitting migraines.

MERCENARY HEELS

We are an army marching the pavement.
We love the clackety-clack sounds we make.

    We nod good-morning-to-you-sir and smile
    the second before we plunge into slush,

leaving behind sopping blasts in our wake.
We swell and puff our chests against cement,

    mud, dog and pigeon poop, and sidewalk cracks.
    Nothing's ever too humiliating.

We are a sisterhood of rubber, nails,
cork, plastic, wood, and a thin coat of paint.

    No matter which cheap country we come from,
    we are all corporate mercenaries.

We owe no allegiance save for humans,
who've easily lost the war to fashion.

CANE-CANE

When I go outside with her, I like to dress up.

            My favorite colors are red, white, and black.

For her blind eyes I dance through my days on pointe.

            I skip splashes like a flat stone across puddles.

I tap left to right, warning of dangerous spots.

            Dancing with my partner is an art.

I love it when everyone can see us coming.

            They wonder how she and I can dance like that.

Gene Kelly in his Technicolor prime can't compare.

            We've outdanced Fred and Ginger to our own music.

Nights I fold up like Audrey Hepburn and sigh.

            I'll always have Paris as long as she keeps me near.

THREADS

Our hips narrowed in the acid glaze of dye,
we sisters braid our slender lives as one
as gnarly fingers, seething wage, loom us
while their machines stitch on designer tags.
After a long trip from home, we are shocked
to find ourselves caressed, fondled, and stroked.
Our lips are sewn shut when she pays thousands
to drape us loosely on her thin shoulders.
We shield our eyes when she struts down the street,
her lacquered nails gripping her Gucci bag,
as a swarm of flashbulbs declare war.
But we're easily forgotten once hung
in the closet where we murmur sadly
before we languish bare in a thrift shop.

GLOVES

We've gone through so much together
since the day we were matched randomly
on an assembly line somewhere

in China. We spent our honeymoon
in a freighter across the Pacific.
Later we found ourselves hanging

among the beggars and tourists
gawking cameras on St. Mark's Place.
We wondered who would adopt us.

One day an old businessman did.
But no one had warned us how
in our marriage we'd still see each other,

hearing each
other breathe,
but never in the same pocket.

OLD MAN CONCRETE

I want to meditate alone, but someone is always
tapping me on the shoulder with their feet,
strollers, bikes, carts of beer, and trashcans.
Sometimes I get banged on with a shovel.
I'm tired of getting blackened with soiled gumballs
and singed from fresh cigarette butts.
It really hurts in winter when I'm peppered
with ice salt and saddled with dog piss.
I'm amazed that I don't have more pockmarks.
My back hasn't cracked either. I'm still alive,
dammit. *Go away all of you*, I want to shout.
The weight of my soul is heavier than my body.
Release me, I pray, of these trappings of my birth.
I long to be reborn as a feather in the heavens.

JUNK MAIL

We wear one *advertiser-approved!* mask
after another, keep our cool for miles
as we leap from box to machines scanning
like salmon fighting to return upstream.
Our faces are stamped with ink upon exit
into the dark echelons of country.
We overhear snippets of dialogue,
soap opera plot twists,
and the steady hum of engine as our swag
at last is carried to our final slots.
Later, we are picked up, ripped, and tossed
into the trash among the broken egg shells
and coffee grounds. Against the falls
of newspaper, our instincts swim up. We must deliver.

LANDFILL

NOISE

We've got a message no one tries to hear.
Humans are still fools to believe in words
and beautifully orchestrated songs.
We are the true spirits of the material world.
We spike sound waves and thrash about,
discordant rumble and clash of chaos
a screeching metal against dulled metal.
Our grunge is only starting to whip chains.
We bong-a-gong in tethered wails and flails
reverberating louder than hollow
garbage cans now jouncing old tumbleweeds
and guitar solos over-wah-wahing.
Prettified words will perish in due time.
We **grunt** and *sigh* and GROAN and *spit* and g r o w l.

FERTILIZER

The serpent that led Eve to taste
the bittersweet knowledge of fruit
has disappeared a long time ago.

Instead, its molten scales have seeped
into the earth, its slick blackness swelling
pure spasms of oil.

White lab-coated men and women
in their microscopic quest for efficiency
have alchemized miracle mixtures.

Thanks to petroleum byproducts,
their uniform gardens achieved yields
barely dreamed of in Eden's time.

People began to require antibiotics.
The eggs of serpent are alive and well.
Greed is the strongest fruit.

CRUCIFIX

If you turned me on my side, I'm a gun
without a trigger. If you held me upside down,
I'm a signpost hammered into the ground.
If you lay me face down, I'm an airport runway.
Face up, I've already turned away from the heavens.
I'm whatever you want to see of me.
I'm an object of no meaning until you pray.

Nobody knows what Jesus looked like.
Yet he's bestowed with a beard, a crown of thorns,
and blunt nails pounded into his palms.
I'm two parts wood to one part metal
poured into a mold in a sweatshop.
I wasn't handmade out of love or piety.
Jesus has left the factory a long time ago.

GARBAGE BAG

I'm big-ass petroleum,
dangerous as your first boyfriend,
drunk and needy with horny promises.

My entire body's leaking fumes.
I miss the uterus of my old life
where no one drilled my pitch-blackness.

I used to be perfectly pleated,
but my stomach is stuffed to the gills
with vegetables, fruits, and packaging.

It's a strange vocation.
I've survived a million years
only to be discarded?

It will take more than a landfill
to suffocate my toxic rage.
I will outlive you and erase your stories.

WASHING MACHINE

I was a blocky cow who chewed its cud in suds.
My steel dentures were bleached clean with toxins.
My stomach had a strong constitution.
Even animals couldn't survive as long.
When humans stuffed my mouth with dirty clothes,
I learned their language of sweat and soil.
They emitted the methane of loneliness.
I allowed clumps of dirt to clog the gaps
between my gnarly teeth. It was a sweet grass,
a longing for the days when I could breathe
free of that basement lit by a sad bulb.
I dreamed of pastures greener in the sun,
a pastoral pond lined with lily pads.
Now I'm junked with other useless dreamers.

CATHODE RAY TUBE

Come cherish my antique televisions
and computer monitors like old friends.
Plasma and LCDs can't last as long
as I have. I'm built solid like a brick.
Technology sissies need not apply.
They worry too much about exposure.
That ridiculous stuff don't mean nothing.
Sure, they say I'm Mr. Radiation:
magnetic fields buzzing with X-ray bands
and toxic phosphors lining my Cyclopean
glass-enveloped eye. I flicker seizures
in photosensitive epileptics
and jackhammer migraines in those who stare.
Come, love, don't be afraid. I'm still healthy.

ATOM

I have nightmares of drowning.
When you're negligible as I am,
even the tiniest drop is an ocean.

My nucleus heart's not even a whisper.
If it were, it'd up and float away
in the big bang of a lover's kiss.

When I listen to people in love,
I long to become a pheromone
unleashing a tsunami of passion.

But molecules are the real stars.
Their combined mass gets them noticed.
I'm just a part of the stage crew.

I'm tired of drifting in the shadows.
Let another lonely atom split my heart in half.
The meek shall inherit the earth.

THE REST OF US

The rest of us objects, disposed of in landfills,
await the day, as seagulls and flies flit
and feast on rotting scraps and carcasses,
when we are no longer made and ignored.
Remaindered, we're just the same old story,
artifacts from when Adam and Eve believed
their creations would rule the universe.

We now canvass the sweet blanket of death,
oozing toxins from our decayed bodies,
once engineered to visual perfection
and celebrated in magazine ads,
with methane steaming upwards to the skies.
Long after humans have perished from making us,
our silences shall sing the final hymn.

ABOUT THE AUTHOR

Raymond Luczak is the author and editor of over 20 books, including seven poetry collections such as *Mute, How to Kill Poetry,* and *The Kiss of Walt Whitman Still on My Lips.* Red Hen Press will bring out his next book *Flannelwood* in the spring of 2019. His work has been nominated nine times for the Pushcart Prize. A playwright, he lives in Minneapolis, Minnesota. [raymondluczak.com]

ABOUT FOMITE

A fomite is a medium capable of transmitting infectious organisms from one individual to another.

"The activity of art is based on the capacity of people to be infected by the feelings of others." —Tolstoy, *What Is Art?*

Writing a review on Amazon, GoodReads, Shelfari, Library Thing or other social media sites for readers will help the progress of independent publishing. To submit a review, go to the book page on any of the sites and follow the links for reviews. Books from independent presses rely on reader to reader communications.

For more information or to order any of our books, visit http://www.fomitepress.com/FOMITE/Our_Books.html

More titles from Fomite ...

Novels
Joshua Amses — *During This, Our Nadir*
Joshua Amses — *Raven or Crow*
Joshua Amses — *The Moment Before an Injury*
Jaysinh Birjepatel — *The Good Muslim of Jackson Heights*
Jaysinh Birjepatel — *Nothing Beside Remains*
David Brizer — *Victor Rand*
Paula Closson Buck — *Summer on the Cold War Planet*
Dan Chodorkoff — *Loisaida*
David Adams Cleveland — *Time's Betrayal*
Jaimee Wriston Colbert — *Vanishing Acts*
Roger Coleman — *Skywreck Afternoons*
Marc Estrin — *Hyde*
Marc Estrin — *Kafka's Roach*
Marc Estrin — *Speckled Vanities*
Zdravka Evtimova — *In the Town of Joy and Peace*
Zdravka Evtimova — *Sinfonia Bulgarica*
Daniel Forbes — *Derail This Train Wreck*
Greg Guma — *Dons of Time*
Richard Hawley — *The Three Lives of Jonathan Force*

Lamar Herrin — *Father Figure*
Michael Horner — *Damage Control*
Ron Jacobs — *All the Sinners Saints*
Ron Jacobs — *Short Order Frame Up*
Ron Jacobs — *The Co-conspirator's Tale*
Scott Archer Jones — *A Rising Tide of People Swept Away*
Julie Justicz — *A Boy Called Home*
Maggie Kast — *A Free Unsullied Land*
Darrell Kastin — *Shadowboxing with Bukowski*
Coleen Kearon — *Feminist on Fire*
Coleen Kearon — *#triggerwarning*
Jan Englis Leary — *Thicker Than Blood*
Diane Lefer — *Confessions of a Carnivore*
Rob Lenihan — *Born Speaking Lies*
Colin Mitchell — *Roadman*
Ilan Mochari — *Zinsky the Obscure*
Peter Nash — *Parsimony*
Peter Nash — *The Perfection of Things*
Gregory Papadoyiannis — *The Baby Jazz*
Andy Potok — *My Father's Keeper*
Kathryn Roberts — *Companion Plants*
Robert Rosenberg — *Isles of the Blind*
Fred Russell — *Rafi's World*
Ron Savage — *Voyeur in Tangier*
David Schein — *The Adoption*
Lynn Sloan — *Principles of Navigation*
L.E. Smith — *The Consequence of Gesture*
L.E. Smith — *Travers' Inferno*
L.E. Smith — *Untimely RIPped*
Bob Sommer — *A Great Fullness*
Tom Walker — *A Day in the Life*
Susan V. Weiss — *My God, What Have We Done?*
Peter M. Wheelwright — *As It Is On Earth*
Suzie Wizowaty — *The Return of Jason Green*

Poetry
Anna Blackmer — *Hexagrams*
Antonello Borra — *Alfabestiario*
Antonello Borra — *AlphaBetaBestiaro*
David Cavanagh — *Cycling in Plato's Cave*
James Connolly — *Picking Up the Bodies*
Greg Delanty — *Loosestrife*

Mason Drukman — *Drawing on Life*
J. C. Ellefson — *Foreign Tales of Exemplum and Woe*
Tina Escaja — *Caida Libre/Free Fall*
Anna Faktorovich — *Improvisational Arguments*
Barry Goldensohn — *Snake in the Spine, Wolf in the Heart*
Barry Goldensohn — *The Hundred Yard Dash Man*
Barry Goldensohn — *The Listener Aspires to the Condition of Music*
R. L. Green — *When — You Remember Deir Yassin*
Kate Magill — *Roadworthy Creature, Roadworthy Craft*
Tony Magistrale — *Entanglements*
Andreas Nolte — *Mascha: The Poems of Mascha Kaléko*
Sherry Olson — *Four-Way Stop*
David Polk — *Drinking the River*
Janice Miller Potter — *Meanwell*
Joseph D. Reich — *Connecting the Dots to Shangrila*
Joseph D. Reich — *The Hole That Runs Through Utopia*
Joseph D. Reich — *The Housing Market*
Joseph D. Reich — *The Derivation of Cowboys and Indians*
Kennet Rosen and Richard Wilson — *Gomorrah*
Fred Rosenblum — *Vietnumb*
David Schein — *My Murder and Other Local News*
Harold Schweizer — *Miriam's Book*
Scott T. Starbuck — *Industrial Oz*
Scott T. Starbuck — *Hawk on Wire*
Seth Steinzor — *Among the Lost*
Seth Steinzor — *To Join the Lost*
Susan Thomas — *The Empty Notebook Interrogates Itself*
Susan Thomas — *In the Sadness Museum*
Paolo Valesio and Todd Portnowitz — *Midnight in Spoleto*
Sharon Webster — *Everyone Lives Here*
Tony Whedon — *The Tres Riches Heures*
Tony Whedon — *The Falkland Quartet*
Claire Zoghb — *Dispatches from Everest*

Stories
Jay Boyer — *Flight*
Michael Cocchiarale — *Still Time*
Michael Cocchiarale — *This Is Ware*
Neil Connelly — *In the Wake of Our Vows*
Catherine Zobal Dent — *Unfinished Stories of Girls*
Zdravka Evtimova — *Carts and Other Stories*
John Michael Flynn — *Off to the Next Wherever*

Derek Furr — *Semitones*
Derek Furr — *Suite for Three Voices*
Elizabeth Genovise — *Where There Are Two or More*
Andrei Guriuanu — *Body of Work*
Zeke Jarvis — *In A Family Way*
Jan Englis Leary — *Skating on the Vertical*
Marjorie Maddox — *What She Was Saying*
William Marquess — *Boom-shacka-lacka*
Gary Miller — *Museum of the Americas*
Jennifer Anne Moses — *Visiting Hours*
Martin Ott — *Interrogations*
Jack Pulaski — *Love's Labours*
Charles Rafferty — *Saturday Night at Magellan's*
Ron Savage — *What We Do For Love*
Fred Skolnik— *Americans and Other Stories*
Lynn Sloan — *This Far Is Not Far Enough*
L.E. Smith — *Views Cost Extra*
Caitlin Hamilton Summie — *To Lay To Rest Our Ghosts*
Susan Thomas — *Among Angelic Orders*
Tom Walker — *Signed Confessions*
Silas Dent Zobal — *The Inconvenience of the Wings*

Odd Birds
Micheal Breiner — *the way none of this happened*
J. C. Ellefson — *Under the Influence*
David Ross Gunn — *Cautionary Chronicles*
Andrei Guriuanu — *The Darkest City*
Gail Holst-Warhaft — *The Fall of Athens*
Roger Leboitz — *A Guide to the Western Slopes and the Outlying Area*
dug Nap— *Artsy Fartsy*
Delia Bell Robinson — *A Shirtwaist Story*
Peter Schumann — *Bread & Sentences*
Peter Schumann — *Charlotte Salomon*
Peter Schumann — *Faust 3*
Peter Schumann — *Planet Kasper, Volumes One and Two*
Peter Schumann — *We*

Plays
Stephen Goldberg — *Screwed and Other Plays*
Michele Markarian — *Unborn Children of America*

Essays
Robert Sommer — *Losing Francis*

www.ingramcontent.com/pod-product-compliance
Lightning Source LLC
Chambersburg PA
CBHW071742080526
44588CB00013B/2130